Jumbled mind mess

Alana Ellis

Presentation by *BookLeaf Publishing*

Web: www.bookleafpub.com

E-mail: info@bookleafpub.com

ISBN: 9789357440165

First edition 2023

When bad times come

When bad times come,
when good times fade,
when tears are shed,
smiles are led away,
there's always someone who cares,
they are there to comfort you,
when bad times come.

When bad times come,
I call on his name,
he doesn't answer in words,
but with friends who love,
and family that cares,
this is who I call on
when bad times come.

When bad times come,
I don't let them stay,
I simply say...
God, push them away.

Love

Love is like a flower
nurture it to grow
no water, but a hug
no sunshine, but kindness
love is special;
happiness and delight,
until it ends
letting it die.

Mind

The mind is such a mystery.
So full of memories stored;
just inside its files.

The mind is such a mystery.
So easy to hold us captive,
with its fascinating workings.
Yet, so hard to get free,
from its constant overthinking.

The mind is such a mystery.
Getting us ever so lost,
in the sadness, darkness and pain.
Letting us forget the enjoyment
of living our beautiful life.

Gone

The light in my eyes,
the spark in my soul,
the day you left
is the day I die.

Not just a piece,
but my whole self.
Just a bag of bones,
with nothing inside.

Just one more day,
just one more talk.
More wisdom words,
a hug around my neck.

My mind is dark,
and my heart is closed.
Moving robotically
because it can't be real.

A lonely place for me,
never the same feeling,
but always the same dealing.
With you gone its
not worth my healing.

Sad

Yesterday I was happy,
today I am sad,
nothing is as planned.
My heart takes a beating,
and I don't understand.
Why I am not hardened
by the cruelty I face?
Maybe I like the abuse?
Because I keep going back,
Just to be used.

I am

I am loving and kind
Wonder why the world is cruel
I hear the laughter all around
See the love in others' souls
I want to be understood
I am loving and kind.

I imagine the day I see heaven
Feel lonely and alone
I touch my friends' lives
Worry about future generations
I cry thinking of my children
I am loving and kind

I understand life is unfair
Life will get better, one day
I dream of a happy future
Try to think positive
I hope to make a difference
I am loving and kind.

Sunset

7

Sunset
Red, orange
Sinking, darkening, cooling
The busy sky sleeps
Dusk

Untitled

Reddened and limp
Your skin is warm
Both dripping sweat
Heart halting hysteria
Breathe
Breathe
Lay with me tonight
Stay with me tomorrow

Morning rises

Mouths talking,
parents fighting,
birds flying in the misty fog.
Hurrying, hurrying,
to catch yellow busses.
Cars passing,
stop lights flashing,
this is what it's like when morning rises.
It's a full moon night,
that leaves me in fright,
for the little deer.
Running, running,
around the woods.
With paper turning,
friends laughing,
people driving,
A man walking on slippery walkways,
stepping Over water puddles.
This is what it's like when morning leaves.

Shyness

Afraid to open up
Never knowing how to act
Uncertain about everything
Shyness is a jail cell.

Broken

11

My heart is held together,
With stitches and staples,
tape and bandages.
It's been beaten, broken,
and bruised.
Despite it all
I still love like it's whole.

Jumbled mess

Jumbled mess
Inside my head.
What is true?
What is false?

Tear stains
On my cheeks,
Over losing me,
Losing my life.

Darkness inside
My blue eyes.
When will it come?
When will it end?

I used to be
Happy, strong.
Now I am not
Worth anything.

Death

Death is a part of life,
A fundamental truth.
We all know it's coming,
Never knowing when.
Think about it often,
Especially as we age.
When will it happen?
Will anybody come?
A morbid fascination,
That's a part of life.

We spend our lives dying,
Never remembering to live.
Forgetting to share our love
With the closest ones to us.
Death is a part of life,
A fundamental truth.
We can never be sure,
Who will be there in the end.

Hated

You've hated me
Since before I was born.
You destroyed me
Before you even saw my face.
You broke me
When I was a fetus
In my mother's womb.
You made it clear,
I was not wanted
Or welcomed in your home.
You belittled
And chastised me
Before I even knew,
And you wonder why,
I haven't respect for you.
You dispised, disregarded
And disowned,
And you expect an
Apology from whom?
Survey not me;
Who was brought into
The world all alone,
To a broken home.
Well guess old man...
Now I am grown.

I donr need your voice in me
Criticizing and lying.
I became who I am
Despite you and
My broken home.
And whe you realized
You were all alone
It was to late
To reach out.
Just remember
The time you had
To be a man.
Decided to chose
Hate everyday.
One day you'll
Hear about me
And know you
Had nothing to
Do with me.

Mama

You knew me so well,
My ride or die for life.
You have always seen me,
The good,bad and in between.
You loved me through it all.
My biggest fan and advocate,
My rock and soft place to land.

Now you are gone
And I am lost, broken.
My biggest fan and confidant,
My first love, the one
That mattered thr most.
I don't know if I'll survive,
But I'll do my very best.

Mama, I miss you.
But know you're here,
In my heart and head.
Watching from there
Cheering my accomplishments,
Guiding and protecting.
'Cause a mothers love
Reaches from the other side.

Love

Such a crazy ride.
Fear and courage,
Pain and happiness
All in one.

Fear of rejection.
Not being enough,
Or being to much.

Courage to go one.
Put yourself out,
In the game, again.

Happiness to be
With someone who,
Who sees you.

Pain from heartache.
Knowing it was
Just a facade.

Such a crazy ride.
Fear and courage,
Pain and happiness,
All in one.

Life

We are meant
To keep evolving.
Changing always,
To keep from
Going old.
Like the ocean,
With every
Ebb and flow.
Life is just
One big
Ripple effect.
Pulling us in,
Pushing us out.
Till we sink,
Or learn to swim.

Loss

I sit here,
Watching.
All these lives
That you have
Unknowingly touched.

I sit here,
Wondering.
Can they feel
The unnatural quiet,
As we laugh?

I sit here,
Knowing.
The pain
Is still here,
Just not as direct.

I sit here,
Listening.
The music,
Being played. Feeling
It's not the same.

Watching, guiding,

Seeing.
The scars,
Are still here,
In all the hearts.

Must we go on?
Emptied,
Emotionally, inside.
The sudden loss
Of our friend.

Depressed

Cut my life in pieces.
In my head, in my head.
Why do I let you get me?
I want it to be over.
Who have I become?
I look in the mirror,
But don't recognize
The person looking back.

Cut my life in pieces.
In my head, in my head.
My own personal prison.
Broke my soul, my peace
And my security.
No longer strong.
Afraid of every look.

Cut my life in pieces.
In my head, in my head.
Make it all stop.
The pain, the noise
And all the words.
I'm the destruction of me.

Love me

I wanted you then
And I still do,
But life has changed
And I'm more afraid
That I won't survive.

My heart is a little
More fragile these days.
I love like it's not
And give like I've
Got nothing to lose.

The reality is,
I don't really know
That I have the fight
To even try because
That's all Ive ever done.
Always the fighter,
Not the fought for.

I wanted you then
And I still do,
But life has changed
And I'm more afraid
That I won't survive.

Stong

You want to hurt me,
With the things you do.
You want to see me break,
With how far you will push.
I've been through hell
And back; and back again.
I've been abused a million ways,
And a million more.
I have survived everything.
Make me cry, break my heart,
Kick me while I'm down.
Give it your best shot,
But remember I am strong.
I was built to survive.

www.ingramcontent.com/pod-product-compliance
Lightning Source LLC
LaVergne TN
LVHW050306200726
843509LV00015B/3192